W9-BRZ-377

April Fool's Day

By Melissa Schiller

Consultant
Don L. Curry
Reading and Content Consultant

Children's Press®
A Division of Scholastic Inc.
New York   Toronto   London   Auckland   Sydney
Mexico City   New Delhi   Hong Kong
Danbury, Connecticut

Designer: Herman Adler Design
Photo Researcher: Caroline Anderson
The photo on the cover shows a girl playing an April Fool's Day
joke on a classmate.

Library of Congress Cataloging-in-Publication Data

Schiller, Melissa.
  April Fool's Day / by Melissa Schiller.
      p. cm. – (Rookie read-about holidays)
  Summary: Introduces the history of April Fools' Day and explains how it
  is observed today.
    ISBN 0-516-25858-3 (lib. bdg.)   0-516-27942-4 (pbk.)
    1. April Fools' Day–Juvenile literature. [1. April Fools' Day. 2.
  Holidays.] I. Title. II. Series.
    GT4995.A6S35 2003
    394.262–dc21
                                      2003000462

CHILDREN'S PRESS, and ROOKIE READ-ABOUT®,
and associated logos are trademarks and or registered trademarks
of Scholastic Library Publishing. SCHOLASTIC and associated
logos are trademarks and or registered trademarks of Scholastic Inc.
1 2 3 4 5 6 7 8 9 10 R 12 11 10 09 08 07 06 05 04 03

Do you celebrate (SEL-uh-brate) April Fool's Day?

April 2004

Sunday	Monday	Tuesday	Wednesday	Thursday	Friday	Saturday
				1	2	3
4	5	6	7	8	9	10
11	12	13	14	15	16	17
18	19	20	21	22	23	24
25	26	27	28	29	30	

The first day of April is called April Fool's Day.

On this day, we make jokes with friends and have fun.

The jokes on April Fool's Day are not meant to harm anyone.

The best jokes are the ones that make everyone laugh.

In France, New Year's used to be celebrated for eight days, starting on March 25. April 1st was the last day of the celebration.

March 2004

Sunday	Monday	Tuesday	Wednesday	Thursday	Friday	Saturday
	1	2	3	4	5	6
7	8	9	10	11	12	13
14	15	16	17	18	19	20
21	22	23	24	25	26	27
28	29	30	31			

April 2004

Sunday	Monday	Tuesday	Wednesday	Thursday	Friday	Saturday
				1	2	3
4	5	6	7	8	9	10
11	12	13	14	15	16	17
18	19	20	21	22	23	24
25	26	27	28	29	30	

People visited one another
and gave gifts.

Then the calendar was changed. January 1st became the start of the new year.

A person who still celebrated New Year's on April 1st was called an "April Fool."

11

In France, April 1st is called "Poisson d'Avril." This means "April Fish."

Children tape paper fish to each other's back. When the paper fish is found, they yell "April Fish!"

People in America first
celebrated April Fool's
Day in the 1800s.

Teachers played along, too.
The teacher would point
up to the sky and say,
"Look! A flock of geese!"

If anyone looked up,
everyone would say,
"April Fools!"

15

In England, jokes are played only in the morning. Some said it was bad luck to play jokes after noon.

If a joke is played on you, you are a "noodle."

17

In Scotland, you are
called an "April gowk."
Gowk is another name
for a cuckoo bird.

In Portugal, April Fool's Day is celebrated on a Sunday.

People throw flour at their friends.

People from all over the world can share the fun by email.

It is exciting to receive funny emails on April Fool's Day.

Newspapers celebrate
April Fool's Day, too.
They print silly articles
(AR-ti-kuhls) as a joke.

Did you read about the
flying pigs?

April Fools!

23

Some people do things backward on April Fool's Day.

They may even eat dessert first!

Then they will say, "April Fools!"

April Fool's Day can be fun.

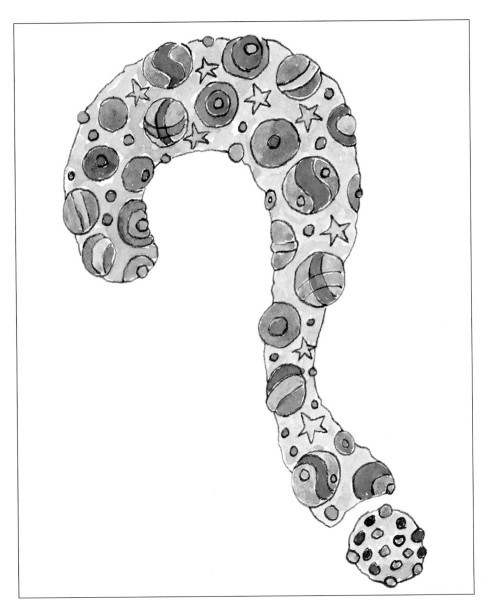

How do you celebrate
April Fool's Day?

Words You Know

article

cuckoo

dessert

email

gifts

jokes

noodle

"Poisson d'Avril"

Index

About the Author

Melissa Schiller taught elementary school for five years and has written a number of children's books. She lives in New York City and has two sons, ages two and four, who are her inspiration for writing.

Photo Credits

Photographs © 2003: Corbis Images: 24, 30 bottom left (LWA/Sharie Kennedy), 7, 31 top right (Tom & Dee Ann McCarthy), 20, 30 bottom right (Thomas Ropke); Ellen B. Senisi: cover; PhotoEdit/Myrleen Ferguson Cate: 9, 31 top left; Stock Boston/John Lei: 17, 31 bottom left; Stone/Getty Images/Paul Harris: 15; Superstock, Inc./Florian Franke: 3; The Image Works/Topham: 18, 30 top right.

Illustrations by Paul Rowntree